Sylvia D. Or  ruw

Happy Birthi   1998.

.enew by date shown.
   ⁻t:

NORFOLK

A Photographic History 1860–1960

A very fine study of Samuel and William Jarvis's 'Victoria Stores' baker's and grocery shop in the village of Terrington St Clement near King's Lynn, *c.* 1900.

NORFOLK

A Photographic History 1860–1960

NEIL R. STOREY

SUTTON PUBLISHING

First published in the United Kingdom in 1996 by
Sutton Publishing Limited · Phoenix Mill · Thrupp · Stroud · Gloucestershire

British Library Cataloguing in Publication Data

A catalogue record for this book is available from the British Library.

ISBN 0-7509-1306-1

Photograph, page 1: John Hewitt of Gimingham, *c.* 1910; page 3: Sidney Grapes (1885–1958). A true Norfolk character and dearly remembered rustic comedian at local concerts and dinners, Sidney is most affectionately remembered for his Boy John letters sent to the *Eastern Daily Press* from 1946 until his death in 1958.

Typeset in 11/15 Baskerville.
Typesetting and origination by Sutton Publishing Limited.
Printed in Great Britain by Butler and Tanner, Frome, Somerset.

This book is dedicated to
Freddie 'Applejack' Gibbons
Keep yew a'troshin' ol' partner

The tableau of 'A Midsummer Night's Dream' at Downham Market carnival in the 1930s.

The ruins of Castle Acre Priory, photographed in about 1905 by Herbert Cave of Dereham. The priory was founded by William de Warrenne, Earl of Surrey, in 1085. It was dissolved in the 1530s by order of King Henry VIII.

INTRODUCTION

Of the traditional counties of England, Norfolk was the fourth largest, covering a total land mass of over 1,300,000 acres or 2,054 square miles. It was slightly expanded after the local government reorganizations of 1974 to take in about 9,000 acres from north-east Suffolk. The county now comprises seven districts: Breckland; Broadland; Great Yarmouth; North Norfolk, Norwich; South Norfolk; King's Lynn and West Norfolk. The coastline of over 90 miles of marshland and dunes is occasionally interrupted by cliffs, as at Hunstanton and Cromer; those in the Weybourne and Sidestrand belt suffer particularly from erosion, resulting from the constant battle against the waves. The county is generally low-lying, crossed and drained by the Rivers Wensum, Yare and Bure with their respective tributaries running into the North Sea, except the north-west corner which is drained by the Ouse into the Wash.

Paleolithic, Mesolithic and Neolithic artefacts have been recovered across the county, dating its first settlers to a period some four to five hundred thousand years ago. The transition from the Neolithic to the Bronze Age occurred about 1700 BC. Remnants of this culture still mark our landscape, with the great round barrows found across the county. These great burial mounds were mainly erected by the Urn folk of Wessex as they progressed up the Icknield Way. At this time large settlements and communities based on agriculture were just beginning to develop in the county. Shortly after, in about 300 BC, the Iceni entered the county; over a number of years they constructed hill forts such as those at

Narborough, Tasburgh, Warham and Thetford, probably to guard their territory against Belgae raiders.

A few years later the Romans invaded, tackling the Iceni castles and settlements, fighting against them in many a brutal conflict, not least of which was the uprising of AD 60, when the tribe was led by Boudicca, its warrior queen. The fighting came to a bloody end, the Romans victorious, but not without suffering defeat in many of the battles and skirmishes, for the Norfolk man is renowned for standing firm for what he believes, and for his fighting abilities, legendary since this time. To guard against future risings, a signal beacon was erected at Thornham to summon the Ninth Legion from Lincolnshire if needed. The construction of Peddars Way gave the legions a clear path into the tribal areas of the Iceni.

The Roman administrative capital was *Venta Icenorum* (Caister St Edmund) covering 40 acres to the east of the River Tas. Roman rule came to a formal end in AD 410 when the province was left to 'defend itself against the barbarians' and eventually the county of Norfolk became part of the Kingdom of East Anglia.

After the Norman Conquest the Domesday Survey records that Norfolk was one of the most heavily populated and wealthiest regions in England, and so it remained throughout the medieval period. The county's wealth was built on the wool trade. At first the sheep belonged to the demesnes of land-owning barons or to the great religious houses, the wool clip sold in bulk to travelling Flemish or Florentine merchants. These dealers were so rich they worked mostly in cash and frequently paid in advance for the entire production of an estate for twenty years! In this way the landowners mortgaged their flocks and put the capital towards building castles or abbeys.

Norfolk also has a large number of churches; in fact, the county has more medieval churches within its borders than any other county of England. At least 921 were built between the eleventh and sixteenth centuries, and 610 are still in use today.

Until the time of the Reformation, the Pilgrim's Way of the Middle Ages wound across the whole of England, bringing religious travellers from all over the country to Norfolk, with others coming from Europe, as part of their 'Grand Tour' in search of enlightenment. Norfolk was criss-crossed by pilgrimage routes, which connected the numerous shrines scattered across the landscape. Often such religious houses had 'relics' or saints as focal points, with their own stories of miraculous visions, cures or creations. Among these were St John the Baptist's head at Trimmingham, a part of the true Cross of Calvary in the Holy Rood of Broomholm at Bacton, St Walstan of Bawburgh and St Withburga at Dereham. There was even the Good Sword of Winfarthing, enshrined in the church for possessing the remarkable ability to find stolen goods or lose unwanted husbands! The most notable and still extant shrine is the Shrine of Our Lady at Walsingham, known as 'England's Nazareth'. For centuries this was one of the most popular destinations for pilgrimages in England. Every king from Richard I to Henry VIII made the journey; good King Harry even walked it barefoot from Barsham Manor.

Norfolk has a long history of Nonconformity, although its level of toleration has varied greatly over the years. When the Huguenot Walloon weavers settled in Norwich they were allowed to use the Bishop's Chapel, a ruinous building used more as a dovecote than a church, 'full of muck and odure', and even then successive bishops attempted to turn them out, eventually leasing them the church of St Mary the Less in Queen Street for five hundred years.

Dissenter meetings were banned from local churches and confined to private houses, outbuildings and barns until the 1689 Toleration Act, which allowed chapels and meeting houses to be built, specifically to be used for Nonconformist meetings. In the mid-eighteenth century John and Charles Wesley led a revival of Anglican evangelism, holding meets across the county.

As time progressed, chapels and churches were established in every town and village in the county, used for meetings by religious dissenters of all sorts – strict, particular, primitive and reformed – and under all titles – Unitarian, Swedenborgian, Methodist, Baptist and Congregationalist. Some parishes had as many as five separate religious groups meeting within their bounds. Today many of these chapels stand redundant or have been converted into village halls or private homes.

At Weybourne, where the beach runs steeply into the sea, ships can come much more closely in to shore. Throughout history the town has been the point at which prospective invaders have landed to begin their plundering and pillaging, hence the old couplet:

> He that would old England win
> Must at Weybourne Hope begin.

Over the years defences have been put up in an attempt to protect the county. There are castles at Castle Acre, Thetford and, of course, Norwich itself. The city was once defended by being completely walled in, as were Great Yarmouth and King's Lynn. Over time further fortifications were made to coastal areas and access rivers, from those devised by the skilled military engineers of Captain York during the Spanish Armada scares to the defences mounted during the Napoleonic Wars and the more familiar 'pill-box' defences, left dotted across the fields of the county after two world wars.

It must be remembered that not all battles on Norfolk soil have been fought with outsiders. In 1381 peasants and serfs across England rose up in angry response to the imposition of an unpopular poll tax. The rising was predominantly led by Geoffrey Litester who, with an insurgent member of the gentry, Sir Roger Bacon, mustered troops on Mousehold Heath in Norwich and stormed the city. Victorious, the rebels spread themselves too far, attacking large towns and ports across the county. The forces became fragmented, with the main body in the north-eastern corner of the county. Bishop Henry le de Spencer, the war-like Bishop of Norwich, rallied the gentry and acquired mercenaries from the continent, who landed at King's Lynn. With them his army marched from the west and engaged the rebels on North Walsham Heath. A bloody battle ensued. The peasants were no match for the skilled swordsmen and hail of arrows, and retreated to the town where they made their last stand in the footings of the parish church. The ringleaders, if not already dead, were summarily executed. Litester was captured and publicly executed at Norwich Castle, thus ending the Peasants' Revolt in Norfolk.

Almost two hundred years later, in 1549, the men of Norfolk rose up again in protest against enclosures and loss of common lands. Some twenty thousand men were mustered at Wymondham, and led by Robert Kett, they marched on Norwich. When they were refused entry to the city they made camp on Mousehold Heath. Here they drew breath before storming the city and defeating a royal army led by the Marquess of Northampton. A second army was sent under the Earl of Warwick. This was joined by German mercenaries and the combined force took the city, forcing the rebels back to Dussindale (Thorpe St Andrew) where they were finally routed. Robert Kett and his brother William were captured, tried and executed in Norwich, their bodies hung in chains from the castle walls as a warning to others.

It seems this fighting and determined spirit has been passed down through the generations; numerous national heroes originate from the county, from Admiral Lord Nelson, the victor at Trafalgar, to Coxswain Henry Blogg GC of the Cromer lifeboat, the most heavily decorated lifeboatman ever, to Nurse Edith Cavell, the daughter of the vicar of Swardeston, shot in 1915 for helping British soldiers to escape from German hands in Belgium. It is also a fact, but like so many other brave and notable things about the county certainly not bragged about, that during the Second World War five men of the Royal Norfolk Regiment received the nation's highest gallantry award – the Victoria Cross, a record unsurpassed by any other regiment during the war. During that same war three whole battalions of local Territorials, part of the ill-fated British 18th Division, were captured at the fall of Singapore in February 1942. They endured over two and a half years as prisoners of war; many never came home. Col. A.E. 'Flicker' Knights said:

In spite of all the Japanese could do, the brutality of the guards, frequent beatings, humiliation and torture suffered by the men of the 4th, 5th, and 6th Battalions of the Royal Norfolk Regiment they never forgot they were soldiers. It was their steady discipline, inflexible courage through adversity and a native dignity and comradeship unique to Norfolk men that brought them through their horrific ordeal.

Whilst one often recalls 'the good old days', it is necessary to remember that everything was not always cheerful and bright. Lack of the means to be hygienic, and poor sanitation facilities led to widespread and frequently fatal disease, which spread through close-knit communities. When times were hard many ended up in the workhouse; there, as in the family home, it was often the survival of the fittest.

Time marches on and changes continue, and this book records some of the most dramatic and meaningful developments ever experienced by the county and its inhabitants. Some images will be reassuringly familiar, others show scenes that have been altered or lost beyond recall. Gone forever are the 'Herring Heydays', the fleet and the fishergirls. Changed beyond all recognition is life on the farm, where once the whole community helped with the harvest and many drew a living from the land. The turnpikes too have gone, replaced by macadamized main roads. The Beeching Act put paid to many local railway lines and stations, and the canals are so silted up that they are certainly not fit for the mighty black-sailed wherries of yesteryear to navigate.

In many ways this book is a photographic 'memory' of the way Norfolk was. Many of the images captured on old film or glass plate, or produced as postcards, are as clear and sharp as the original views seen through the eyes of the photographers themselves. This is certainly a tribute in itself to their skill.

I hope that this book will go some way to preserving what has passed, and that it will make us all more aware of the history that still remains around us today. We should not be so quick to move forward without looking back and learning from the past.

Neil R. Storey
Norwich
1996

FROM THE CRADLE
TO THE GRAVE

Ernest Culham, the Pulham Market butcher, stands proudly with his family, April 1918.

Staff and clients of Blofield Red Cross Infant Welfare Centre, *c.* 1919. In Norfolk during the 1920s there were only one hundred trained midwives to cover the whole county. Coupled with squalid living conditions and a catalogue of diseases, such as typhoid, scarlet fever and diphtheria, this resulted in the deaths of up to twenty women a year in childbirth, as well as an horrific number of infant mortalities. Welfare organizations such as this, staffed mostly by members of voluntary aid organizations and operated once a month from church halls and rural chapels, were few and far between until after the Second World War and the establishment of the Welfare State.

Washbridge, East Dereham, *c.* 1910. This typical rural settlement of cottages would have shared the communal pump, which had probably been installed over a much earlier sunken well. The very poor sanitation facilities of earth closets, and the 'night soil' heaps, resulted in all manner of effluent seeping into such wells over the years. The untreated water was drunk by all those who drew from the well, causing the rapid spread of diphtheria and cholera, which decimated families. Unfortunately this remained a common fact of life until the 1920s, when most councils started programmes of sewerage improvement and installed piped water supplies for rural areas.

Strumpshaw Urban District (Brandeston and Brundall) Board School, *c.* 1900. The bespectacled Mrs Johnston, the school mistress, keeps a watchful eye at the side of the group. The school was built in 1874.

Students at Little Ellingham Dairy, June 1909. From the end of the nineteenth century there was an increasing move towards education in good farming practice at national and county government level. Therefore a number of local schools hosted 10-day courses, led by a team set up by the Norfolk Technical Education Committee, on special skills such as dairying and poultry-keeping. There was even a series of eight lectures on bee-keeping.

Watts' Naval Training School, North Elmham, *c.* 1910. The building was presented to Dr Barnardo by Sir Fenwick Shadforth Watts as a school for three hundred boys run on the lines of Naval life and discipline. It closed in 1953.

Class 1a, Northgate Boys' School, Great Yarmouth, *c.* 1933. These are first year boys (still in short trousers!) enjoying the benefit of the Hadow Report of 1926, which recommended the segregation of pupils over the age of 11 into separate schools, and thus a 'Secondary' education at secondary or senior schools.

Paston Grammar School football team, North Walsham, *c.* 1912. Places at the school were paid for by the more wealthy families in the area and there were a number of boarders. Local boys with parents of lesser means could attend the school by obtaining scholarships awarded because of good academic performance.

A day remembered well by all children is the school sports day. Note the expressions on the faces of these parents as they watch their children at North Walsham Secondary Modern School Sports Day, 1951.

The Church of St Mary Margaret at Hapton, *c.* 1910. For many years local families would walk a number of miles in their Sunday best to attend such churches, which served widely dispersed rural communities.

'The Happiest Day of Your Life'. The wedding group of Jack Pardon and Phyllis Griffin (the author's great-uncle and aunt), with their parents and bridesmaids, after their marriage at St Nicholas Church, North Walsham, June 1937. Jack and Phyllis honoured the vows they took for the rest of their lives; they were happily married for almost sixty years.

St Mary's Church Choir, Docking, 1907. Centre left of the group is Revd Hugh James Hare MA, Parish Vicar, Chaplain of the Workhouse, Rural Dean of Heacham and Honorary Canon of Norwich.

The bells of St Mary the Virgin Church, Tasburgh, 1900. Standing beside them are, left to right: William Lant Duffield, church warden and local miller; Revd Walter Robert Hurd, the rector; and Philip Berney-Ficklin JP, church warden and one of the principal local landowners. The four original bells were retoned and the treble was a new addition made by Taylors of Loughborough.

The Revd Augustine Brutton MA stands proudly beside his bicycle in front of Hempnall Vicarage, along with his family and servants, 1905. Once every village and town had its own vicar and rectory. A sad reflection of the times is that now most of the rectories have been sold off and the smaller groups of villages put together in 'team parishes', sharing one itinerant vicar. (Photo, Philip Standley)

The bunting is up and no doubt this group of children are eager to enjoy the tea party and celebrations hosted by the vicar of Marham in the vicarage garden after the consecration of the new extension to the churchyard on 6 June 1911.

Preachers and congregation of Dilham Primitive Methodist Chapel, *c.* 1910. Norfolk has a long-·standing reputation for Nonconformity. Congregations had to meet in barns and houses until the 1689 Toleration Act when they were allowed to build their own religious houses. Chapels sprang up right across the county, with some parishes having as many as five different religious groups meeting within their bounds.

Dereham Road (Norwich) Primitive Methodist Sunday schools treat, *c.* 1908. Once a year in the summer months the various Sunday schools across the county would have an outing. To transport the children local traders would lend their trade carts, each with gaily painted sides showing the various businesses. The children wore their Sunday best and took flags to wave, so it made quite a spectacle. (Photo, Basil Gowen)

The Church Army van at Morley St Botolph, *c.* 1905. The Church Army took the idea of open-air preaching, popularized by the Methodists, one stage further. With their fully equipped caravans, which included hymn sheets, Bibles and a harmonium, they travelled around villages holding 'camp meetings' on village greens. (Photo, Philip Standley)

North Walsham Salvation Army Band, *c.* 1947. The Salvation Army has a long tradition of service in Norfolk. Since the latter part of the nineteenth century meetings have been held in the Army's halls in villages and towns across the county. Often entire families would be members of the same branch, following in the footsteps of previous generations.

No.1 (Great Yarmouth) Voluntary Aid Detachment. The British Red Cross Society ambulance and crew, *c.* 1919. Until 1970, when the Norfolk Ambulance Service was established in its own right, the responsibility of transporting casualties rested on the shoulders of organizations such as the British Red Cross Society and St John Ambulance. Even in the early days their transport was often out of date – old corporation vehicles or private cars and lorries paid at a rate of 3*d* a mile!

Town dignitaries take part in the dedication ceremony of Holt's new St John Ambulance on the afternoon of Sunday 29 May 1938. Among the guests standing on the dais are Mr R.J. Colman, the Lord Lieutenant, Viscount Bury, Lord and Lady Cozens-Hardy, along with senior St John officers. The Revd Herbert King, rector of Holt, conducted the dedication service. The ambulance was paid for entirely by charitable donations and fund-raising over the previous eighteen months.

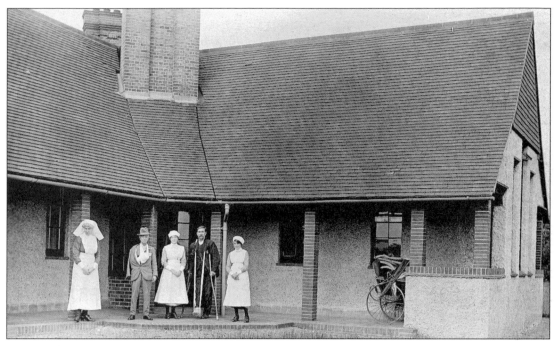

Wells Cottage Hospital, *c.* 1920. The hospital was erected in 1910 by the Holkham tenantry as a memorial to the 2nd Earl of Leicester KG. It originally provided six beds and two cots and was staffed by nurses and members of the local British Red Cross Society.

Officials and farm workers who had received long service awards at the Fakenham Show, August 1939. Their total cumulative service amounted to over 375 years.

Presentation of a mantle clock for long service in the South Lopham Temperance League, *c.* 1895. Such 'friendly societies' were spread throughout the county; some promoted temperance or Christian ideals, while others mainly offered mutual assistance in old age and times of need before the days of state pensions and welfare.

The Union Workhouse at Downham Market, *c.* 1905. Built with this distinctive brick and ragstone design in 1836 at a cost of about £5,000, the workhouse was situated some distance from the main towns and villages that it would serve. At a time when life was perhaps more difficult than it is today, it was a common occurrence to end up 'on the parish', and the workhouse could accommodate some 250 inmates. Such institutions, each with its Board of Governors who appointed the master and matron, would be responsible for housing, feeding and providing work for the unemployed or destitute of the parish. Although the food was good and wholesome, the discipline and division of families into male, female and children's quarters seems strict and harsh. (Photo, Philip Standley)

The sisters of Trinity Hospital, Castle Rising, *c.* 1930. The sisters are wearing their distinctive steeple hats and red cloaks, which bear the badge of Henry Howard, Earl of Northampton, who founded the 'hospital' of twelve Bede houses for ladies '. . . to be 56 years of age at least; no common beggar, harlot, scold, drunkard, haunter of taverns, inns or ale-houses'. The sisters were also sworn to endeavour to live peaceably with one another.

Residents of the Fishermen's Hospital, Market Place, Great Yarmouth, *c.* 1930. Founded in 1702, this was home to twenty disabled and aged fishermen who had reached the age of sixty or over.

The opening of the Almshouses on Diss Common by HRH Edward the Prince of Wales in 1867. The local Rifle Volunteers, militia and civic dignitaries along with this huge crowd turned out for the occasion. The Almshouses were to become home to thirteen local elderly couples and widows. Such schemes, a precursor to sheltered housing, were popular across the county and built by local boards or charities using legacies left for the purpose.

On 22 October 1910 the *Heathfield*, loaded with coal, was wrecked off Cley. Eight sailors lost their lives, and were buried at Wells. Seen here near the mortuary are the coffins of the two Roman Catholic sailors. As there was no Roman Catholic church nearby, the coffins were carried in procession by men from the maltings for a makeshift service held in the Eight Ringers public house on Church Plain. (Photo, Eric Reading)

Keep Yew A'Troshin'

Top Farm in the village of Thompson, 1915. The population here at the time was 358; I wonder if the ducks outnumbered the residents?

The first Monday after the Feast of Epiphany was known as 'Plough Monday', when the ploughmen would set their teams of horses to the fields. Pictured here is a scene near Hevingham in 1903; the farming year has begun. (Photo, Philip Standley)

A Norfolk ploughman filling his seed drill, 1953. Although seed drills had been around for over two hundred years, they were slow to become popular. Only a few years before this photograph was taken seeds would have been sown by broadcast sowing. The drill shown here was made by Smith and Son of Peasenhall, Suffolk. Gearing attached to the wheels picked up the seeds and dropped them down pipes penetrating the earth. It was then covered over by the small hoes set behind.

Wheat dibbling at Hethersett, *c.* 1910. The dibblers walked backwards making a hole every 3 to 4 inches, which was then filled with seed by those who followed. This job was often done by the elderly and children, who earned themselves 6*d* a day.

Jimmy Davison, the vermin destroyer of Swanton Abbot, netting sparrows, *c.* 1925. Known as the 'King of the Molecatchers', Jimmy worked the local farms for many years. All animals caught were skinned, their pelt often made into tippets, a type of hand muff. The carcasses were hung along fences to show how many had been caught. Apparently nothing was wasted in those days, and even sparrow pie was a popular country dish.

Norwich horse fair on Bell Avenue, *c.* 1908. Such fairs were traditionally held on Ascension Day in May and were popular events at a time when the horse was a driving force in the country. Servants could also be hired at the fairs and at the end of the day came the 'Rogation Gangings' – great celebrations when there would be a 'perambulation of beer' and picnic feasting. (Photo reproduced by kind permission of Eastern Counties Newspapers)

Boys driving sheep to pasture, *c.* 1910. Drovers and their boys were once a common sight clogging up country lanes as they drove sheep or cattle to the nearest market, sometimes many miles away. (Photo, Philip Standley)

Sheep-washing at Grazing Ground Farm, Shelton, *c.* 1910. Left to right: Fred Hanner, Arthur Hanner, Herbert Hanner, Robert Hanner, David Hanner and Marshall Hanner. The sheep here are penned before being driven into and dipped into a dammed watercourse to remove insects and impurities from the wool, before shearing.

Sheep pens at Norwich cattle market, *c.* 1930. This market, covering over 8½ acres, existed here from the thirteenth century. When this picture was taken 6 auctioneers and 33 private dealers on the site sold 212,000 head of stock and 100,000 fowl and turkeys per annum, with sales exceeding £1,250,000. At the height of the sales 1,650 beasts were fed and watered here on sale eves. (Photo reproduced by kind permission of Eastern Counties Newspapers)

Pig pens at Fakenham cattle market, *c.* 1930. This market was constructed near Bridge Street in 1857. Weekly stock sales were held on Thursdays at noon, the business conducted by long-established local auctioneers Messrs Long and Beck. Such cattle markets, for centuries an established part of life in the larger county towns of Norfolk, are now, in the main, sadly consigned to the past.

Watton Corn Hall, *c.* 1909. This was part of the Wayland hall, built in Watton market place in 1853 and comprising a corn hall, magistrate's rooms, library and committee rooms. As time passed on so did the trade in corn, and most of the halls came to be used for large local functions, especially boxing matches. Some were even converted into cinemas. (Photo, Philip Standley)

Horace J. Heyhoe's chemist and grocery shop next door to the Crown Hotel in Fakenham market place, *c.* 1905. The premises are decked out for town festivities, the continuing wealth of the land promoted on the emblazoned banner, 'Success to Agriculture'.

A drawing match at Guistwick, 1952. Such competitions were not just a test of speed but of skill in horse management too. Everything on the horses' tack was soaped and polished, braids and bells were woven into the manes and the horses groomed immaculately. The result was a fine sight and can still be seen nowadays at county shows held throughout the summer. (Photo reproduced by kind permission of Norfolk Rural Life Museum)

Frank 'The Guv'nor' Randell with his stand of agricultural machinery at one of the big farming shows, *c.* 1925. For over one hundred years the Randell family firm made such machinery and other implements at their St Nicholas Foundry Works off Bacton Road, North Walsham.

Committee members at the North Walsham, Cromer and Aylsham Triennial Agricultural Show, 1911. Left to right: Ernest Owles, Hall Farm, Gimingham; George Cobon, Old Hall Farm, Witton; William Case, Tuttington Hall, Aylsham; William Allan, Home Farm, Banningham; Col. Harvey Barclay (President), Hanworth Hall; H.G. Oclee; Lt-Col. Benjamin Sapwell of Aylsham; Brereton Page Wood, Morston; Ben Ling, Ashmanhaugh; P. Case of Lamas; and H.F. Proudfoot (Secretary). (Photo, Mike Ling)

Working horses are proudly paraded around the arena at the Royal Norfolk Show, 1950. The Norfolk Show has been held at various venues across the county, the first one on the old Norwich cricket ground in 1849. In 1952 the Royal Norfolk Agricultural Association bought the present 230 acre site at Costessey and since 1954 all Royal Norfolk Shows have been held there.

The Norfolk Federal Union meeting at Swanton Morley sandpit to celebrate George Rix's success in the Vestry elections of 1876. Unfortunately for Mr Rix, it was a false victory as, although he received the most individual votes, the farmers' plural votes carried the day. After the event, copies of this photograph were sold for 2*s* each, proceeds going to union funds.

An election meeting at East Rudham, 1918. In the cart are, left to right, George Hewitt, leader of the 1910 St Faith's strike; Tom Higden, the Burston schoolmaster; 'General' Robert Walker, socialist secretary; George Chapman; George Edwards, the Labour candidate and notable local union leader; James Arnett; unknown; unknown.

The Great Agricultural Labourers' Strike, 16 April 1923. Two hundred agricultural labourers march down Wicklewood High Street on their way to the rally at Kimberley Park, where the chair was taken by the Earl of Kimberley, the first peer to declare himself a Labour Party supporter.

Strawberry pickers at Failes Farm, Tilney All Saints, *c.* 1905. A pleasant summer activity nowadays is to 'pick your own' strawberries, a far cry really from the days when everyone 'pitched in' to harvest the ripe fruit, which was then sent on by the train-load to the city and markets across the country. In this case the fruit was trotted the mile to Clenchwarton station by pony and cart.

Local ladies with their printed aprons and sun-hats are drafted in as currant pickers at Banningham, July 1923. They are pictured here with the regular male farm-hands.

Potato pickers at Outwell, *c.* 1910. The crop was spun out of the ground by a horse-drawn potato lifter, picked up and put in baskets by hand and then taken to the waiting carts. Although it was a poorly paid and thankless task, it was welcomed by the farm workers as a means of gaining a little extra income before the winter set in.

Dutchmen raising sugar beet at Bracon Ash, *c.* 1907. It was quite common to see foreign workers in the county. They came over from Ireland and Holland early in the year to plant potatoes, and stayed on to hoe mangels and swedes, and to harvest hay and corn. They would return home after the sugar beet was lifted, which would probably have been the last harvest of the farming year. Often the final cart-loads of beet would be brought in after the new year had begun.

Scythe harvesters gathering in the barley at Ellingham, *c.* 1890. When the scythe gangs were assembled for the first time in the new season they would appoint a 'hainer' or 'harvest lord' to negotiate their wages with the farmer. When harvesting, the hainer led the men in an extended line across the fields; when he stopped, everyone else would stop, and not before!

Pausing for a drink during harvesting at Laurel's Farm, Mundham. To refresh the harvesters, drinks would be brought out to them in the fields. Cold tea was drunk for the first part of the day, known as 'dew drink' first thing in the morning, ''levenses' at mid-morning and 'noonings' at lunchtime. In the afternoon the final drink of the day, 'fourses' or 'bevers', was usually good strong local beer, which is what the men in the photograph are enjoying. Everyone in the picture worked the field; the scythemen harvested, some of the children and older men raked the mown hay, and the smallest children hunted the mice and rabbits chased out by the harvesters.

A sail reaper on a south Norfolk farm, *c.* 1895. The days of the scythe harvest were numbered with the introduction of this machine. As the reaper was drawn along, the sails spun round cutting the corn and sweeping it behind, where it was raked and gathered into sheaves by hand.

A horse-drawn hay cutter, *c.* 1908. Hidden beneath the crop is the reciprocating cutter bar; the cut grass would drop in broad swathes to be raked by the labourer following the machine. Such a mowing system could mow an acre in one hour – a day's task for a skilled scytheman.

Frederick Griffin (the author's great-grandfather), farm foreman at River Farm, Honing, on his binder pulled by a magnificent team of Suffolk Punch horses, *c.* 1925. The binder/harvester was the final nail in the coffin for the manual harvesters – both the scythemen and the teams who followed them, tying up the sheaves. This machine not only reaped but also bound sheaves automatically, cutting an average of 8 acres of corn a day. When such machinery was first introduced sporadic instances of machine sabotage occurred but little could stand in the way of progress.

The threshing team near Fakenham, taking a break from their 'troshin'' or feeding the thresher, *c.* 1906. The cleaned corn would emerge from the end of the thresher closest to the steam engine and was immediately put into waiting sacks, while the straw emerged from the opposite end. Such machinery was more often than not hired from local contractors; the traction engine rattling and hissing along country lanes, towing the elevator and drum, was a common sight during harvest time.

Norfolk rickyard, *c.* 1900. Wagons piled high were drawn alongside the new rick and the men on the wagon would pitch the loose hay to the man on top of the rick. Over the following weeks the hay would settle under its accumulated weight and only then could the top be skilfully thatched to make a weatherproof cover.

The 'Horkey' load, *c.* 1920. This was the last load of hay gathered in and it was sent round the neighbouring farms to mock those who had not yet reaped down their harvest. This load was traditionally paraded round the village doused with water to signify that all was safely gathered in so the rains could begin. (Photo, George Hill)

The Norfolk Post Windmill at Wreningham, when kept by Harry Andrews, the steam and wind miller, *c.* 1900. Many such mills, peculiar to this county, have dotted the skyline for hundreds of years. Their popularity waned as brick tower mills with larger capacity and easier maintenance were developed. (Photo, Philip Standley)

Right: Hindolveston tower mill, *c.* 1910.
Built in 1844 by John Pegg, the mill was
let in 1906 to Mrs Agnes Bowman, who
also kept the village post office. The
business was carried on into the 1930s by
the Davidson family. Eventually the mill
fell into disrepair and was partially
dismantled. It is now a private residence.

Below: Harvest Festival at North
Walsham church rooms, *c.* 1909.
Celebrations both religious and bawdy
have traditionally been associated with
the successful gathering in of the harvest
and in the days of the scythemen the
'Harvest Horkey', best described in the
old Norfolk rhyme:

> Heed ye not the uncouth lingo,
> Quick the polished spit display,
> Broach the cask of nut brown stingo,
> Harvest home's a holiday.

The final job after the harvest was to plough the land in order to bury the remains of the previous crop. The ground was then rolled to break down and consolidate the new surface and harrowed ready for a new arable season. (Photo, Philip Standley)

Workmen wearing their traditional working clothes of corduroy and 'buskins' (lower-leggings made of leather or canvas) bank the farm trackway near Docking, *c*. 1904. This practice, along with ditching, drainage and hedging, kept the land labourers busy through the winter months, preparing the land for the rigours of the season and ensuring it was fit to serve another farming year.

Albert Trapett returning from a day's ploughing at Etling Green, near East Dereham, on an American made 'Titan' tractor, *c.* 1924. The first experimental tractors appeared on British farms at the turn of the century, but were treated with contempt. However, during the First World War Lloyd George's government, in response to the country's need to maximize food production, ordered six thousand tractors from America. Proving effective, the tractor was eventually adopted as essential farm machinery, replacing the working farm horse by the 1950s.

Harry Burden, the butcher, and his apprentice at Weasenham St Peter, *c.* 1900. At the turn of the century most rural families kept a pig, raising it over the year until Christmas time when the local butcher would be called upon to slaughter it to supply the family with winter fare.

Plucking Norfolk turkeys, 1893. The light land area of south-west Norfolk has always been renowned for turkeys of peculiar size and delicacy and great numbers are reared every year. In days gone by, during the period before Christmas, many travellers were inconvenienced by the coaches heading for London loaded full of crates of turkeys, bound for the city markets.

HIGHWAYS & BYWAYS

Robert Brown, aged seventy-two, riding a wooden tricycle made by James Patteson of Foxley in 1875, pictured on the Bawdeswell Road, Foxley, in August 1915. (Photo reproduced by kind permission of Norwich Central Library)

Turnpike road at Swardeston, running by the Dog Inn, *c.* 1905. An Act of Parliament enabled a turnpike trust to operate this route, running from Norwich to New Buckenham, in 1772. Before the days of the turnpike, responsibility for the upkeep of roads fell to the parishes through which they passed, and they were in the main in a terrible state of repair. Turnpike trusts were established as private bodies of investors to finance the upkeep of roads, which they did by setting up toll-gates along the route to collect fees. (Photo, Philip Standley)

Pictured shortly after its establishment in August 1909 is Thomas Cook's Stage Coach Service, in front of the New Inn at Roughton. Known as 'The Lobster', the service ran in the summer months from Cromer via Aylsham, Roughton, Marsham and St Faiths to the Maid's Head Hotel in Norwich. It employed twenty-five ostlers. The service, however, was described as a 'rich man's whimsy' and ceased before the First World War. (Photo, Basil Gowen)

Norfolk County Council road gangers on the Swaffham to Fakenham road at West Lexham, 1912. In 1890 Norfolk County Council began to invest heavily in road maintenance. The budget of the western division of the county totalled £23,610, of which only £500 could be spent on 'improvements' and £300 on tools and equipment to supplement the traditional wheelbarrows, picks and shovels. The remaining money was to be spent on the construction of new roads. In November the eastern division bought a steam roller 'as an experiment' and the mechanization of the road repair service slowly began.

From the 1780s roads were built with a harder macadamized cambered surface of flint, granite and binding silt drawn from local gravel pits. Photographed here during the First World War is the gravel pit at Holt, owned by Arthur Preston. As the men have been called up, women are working the pit.

Sam Marshall, the Wymondham general dealer, *c.* 1905. Sam travelled around the numerous villages surrounding Wymondham selling all manner of hardware from his cart. He was just one of the hundreds of itinerant salesmen who sprang up across the county, taking advantage of the greatly improved road system to spread their business out of town.

Thomas Cross, the coal merchant from Worstead, *c.* 1905. Even the essentials had to be carried by road. Coal used to be landed by cutters on local beaches and either taken by cart to canals for long distance transport or trekked over land to surrounding villages and sold by dealers like Tom. (Photo, Philip Standley)

The improved roads made travelling far more accessible and comfortable, and small trotting carts and traps were popular. Photographed here are ladies of the Hinde family of Pulham Market, enjoying a ride in 1909.

Although horse power was being superseded by the motor car, some clung on to traditional modes of transport, especially in more rural areas. Mr Ralph Wells of Meadow Cottage, White Lion Road, in Coltishall, was roundsman for Roys Coltishall Bakery for fifty years. He is pictured here at Buxton, along with his cart and his horse 'Jolly', shortly before his retirement in September 1962.

Postmen at Scottow post office, *c.* 1907. Transport improvements were certainly welcomed by rural postmen, who often walked many miles over poor roads pulling handcarts with wooden iron-shod wheels. It must have seemed like a Godsend when they were issued with bicycles with pneumatic tyres. (Photo, Philip Standley)

Breakdown recovery engineers from J.J. Wright of East Dereham ready to go to work, *c.* 1920. One problem with early Ford cars was that their axles broke easily, as has happened here. Such accidents in the rut-ridden country lanes of Norfolk were frequent occurrences. (Photo, Terry Davy)

With the increasing number of cars on the road the need for accessible and efficient assistance for maintenance or emergency recovery became a necessity. The Automobile Association set up its offices at the bottom of Thorpe Road shortly after the turn of the century and AA boxes appeared across the county. Smart officers like Bob Eustace, pictured in March 1937 with his Rudge Whitworth bicycle, would snap up a salute to all members displaying the AA badge on their cars. (Photo, Mike Ling)

Gypsy caravans, pictured by local itinerant photographer Tom Nokes, *c.* 1900. These magnificent Reading vans and barrel-topped vardos were home to the true Romany people, epitomized in the writings of the Norfolk-born author George Borrow. They were often seen in the corner of fallow fields or common land, along with small shelters called 'benders', which were simply sticks hooped over and stuck into the ground, and covered with canvas or skins. (Photo, Philip Standley)

Roads have been the scene for, as well as the subject of, many protests over the years. Here at Wymondham in 1909, 'Old Chowes' Blazey parades the roads in mock mourning after the town's Whit Monday sports were called off. He is accompanied by some of the children who joined him en route. (Photo, Philip Standley)

WATERWAYS & BROADS

Wherries at Wayford Bridge, *c.* 1905. Vessels would gather here to ply the length of the North Walsham and Dilham Canal, a navigation which was opened on 29 August 1826. At the opening ceremony local dignitaries were conveyed along the canal in a fine vessel, followed by a second which carried the band. The banks were lined by hundreds of onlookers, who had gathered to admire the spectacle. (Photo, Philip Standley)

Felmingham water mill, *c.* 1905. The present mill, situated on a tributary of the River Bure, has been on the site for about two hundred years. In 1845 it was kept as a corn mill by Richard Hylton. Thomas Gaze, the farmer and miller, owned it at the turn of the century, and in the early 1920s it passed into the hands of the well-known local millers Barclay, Pallett & Co. Ltd. It is now a private house.

Wroxham Bridge, *c.* 1905. The men on board the wherry are in the process of lowering its sail and mast in order to pass under the bridge. Hundreds of wherries plied the Broads and rivers, carrying all manner of cargoes, ranging from coal and timber to corn and sugar beet. Each vessel could carry about 30 tons.

Eel catcher on Wroxham Broad, *c.* 1890. The makeshift hut in the background was constructed on an old boat, and the catcher would live there while he tended his sett. (Photo reproduced by kind permission of Norwich Central Library)

Reed cutting on the River Ant, *c.* 1890. The dry reeds were mown down with scythes, bundled together and piled onto the small boat, or lighter. Even after their hard day's toil, the men would still tow the lighter back to the nearest dry area, where the reeds were stacked. (Photo reproduced by kind permission of Norwich Central Library)

Once the stack got to a decent enough size, the reeds were loaded onto one of the 25 ft 'full load' lighters or a converted wherry hull (as pictured here). The boat was towed, or quanted, up to the nearest staithe. This photograph was taken at Wroxham in 1956; some 450 bundles of reed are being loaded onto a lorry belonging to Farman's, a reed thatcher from North Walsham.

Regatta on Wroxham Broad, *c.* 1890. A successor to the jolly and often drunken chaos of the early nineteenth-century 'water frolics', regattas were often well organized gatherings of yachts. Events included races and demonstrations of navigational skills and of course a chance to moor up, take a picnic from your wicker basket and simply enjoy the spectacle. (Photo reproduced by kind permission of Norwich Central Library)

Yachts sail past Horning ferry in about 1922, when the Ferry Inn was kept by Mark Osborne, who also hired out fishing boats to the area's many visitors. The old horse ferry itself could be traced back to 1246, when it was referred to as Grabbardes's ferry. The ferry ceased working in the late 1930s, but a pedestrian ferry still traverses the river today.

Fishing the waters of the richly stocked Womack Broad, beside the moored pleasure yacht *Mascot*, *c.* 1921. The Broads teemed with fish of all kinds – bream, roach, perch and of course record-breaking pike.

The Broads have been synonymous with hired and touring pleasure craft since the 1880s. Here is an early steam vessel, the *Spitfire*, owned by Boyce F. Shields. Donald Gant and Alfred Woodbright are among those on board, *c.* 1885.

RAILWAYS

Labourers constructing sheds at a Midland & Great Northern (M&GN) Railway goods yard, *c.* 1895.

Stationmaster William Mill and his staff, along with the drivers of the goods train at Brundall Great Eastern Railway (GER) station, pause for the photographer, *c.* 1904. (Photo, Philip Standley)

Swainsthorpe signal-box and men, *c.* 1912. Swainsthorpe was on the GER Victoria line from Diss to Norwich, which opened in 1849. This signal-box became redundant in 1986, and has been transported to the narrow-gauge Wells and Walsingham Railway where it is used as a gift shop. (Photo, Philip Standley)

M&GN Cromer Beach station, *c.* 1895. The GER brought the first railway to Cromer in 1877. Ten years later the M&GN completed their line here at Cromer Beach. By the turn of the century the GER and M&GN Joint Railway (the Norfolk and Suffolk Joint Railway) had built the coastal loop from North Walsham to Mundesley and on to Cromer via Overstrand. The lines had been fraught with financial difficulties and were completed only after funds were raised by local groups of gentry and businessmen. Their investments paid rich dividends as the holiday trade brought by the railways boomed.

The GER station at Coltishall, *c.* 1904. Richard J. Read, his family and the station staff observe the railway gangers maintaining the plates and tracks. (Photo, George Gosling)

M&GN Fakenham Town station and staff, *c.* 1904. Known to locals as 'Hempton station', after the parish in which it was situated, the station was located quite a way out of town. It was built in the 1880s by the Lynn and Fakenham Railway Company, and operated for many years until its closure in the 1950s.

Steaming by Honing sidings, *c.* 1930. This section of track was part of the 41 mile long line running from Great Yarmouth to Melton Constable, founded by the Great Yarmouth & Stalham Railway in the 1880s. When the line was extended to North Walsham passengers were able to travel to Mundesley or on to Cromer and Sheringham in 'Poppyland'. Taken over by the M&GN Railway at the turn of the century, the line was closed to passengers on 28 February 1959.

Things did not always run smoothly on the M&GN (nicknamed the 'Muddle and Go Nowhere'). Here the No. 36 engine has collided with goods wagons at Guestwick on 31 October 1908. William Marriott, the M&GN's ubiquitous engineer and locomotive superintendent (second from the right), supervises the recovery operation.

During the floods of August 1912, Tharston Viaduct was completely washed away by the torrential waters of the River Tas. The following day a gang from Stratford arrived on the scene and rebuilding proceeded at a good pace. This picture, taken in September 1912, shows the brick piers nearing completion. (Photo, Philip Standley)

The Norwich to Great Yarmouth 'Beach Express' steams across the level-crossing just beyond Whitlingham junction on the GER line, *c.* 1929.

The 'Eastern Belle' passing through Whitlingham station, *c.* 1935. With holidays and excursions becoming viable for most people, direct rail services ran non-stop express trains from London to Norfolk's coastal resorts. Great Yarmouth's stations were so busy during the summer holiday peak-times that a train ran every ten minutes to faraway destinations such as Walsall and Derby to pick up holiday-makers.

THE CITY

Panorama of the city of Norwich from Gas Hill, *c.* 1939. Dominating the scene and visible for miles around, as it has been for nine hundred years, is the Cathedral Church of the Holy and Undivided Trinity, founded in 1096 by Herbert de Losinga, the first Bishop of Norwich.

Norwich Castle and cattle market, *c.* 1910. Originally a wooden fortification, the stone keep was erected in about 1160. By the 1290s the city had been entirely walled in, with forty towers and eleven fortified gates, and the importance of the castle as a defensive stronghold greatly diminished. For a time it served as a gaol, until the new prison was built outside the city in 1887, and the castle was purchased by the Norwich Corporation. The keep was converted into a museum.

Herbert Parker's seed stall in front of the Agricultural Hall, *c.* 1900. Originally dealing in coal, corn, cement, dry salter and as a manure merchant, Herbert's seeds were a side line, sold round the corner at the cattle market. However, as this business flourished over the years it became the sole trade of the well-remembered firm of Herbert Parker Ltd at the Tower Wharf on Riverside.

William Clarke's ironmonger's shop, *c.* 1895. This building, built on the side of the Bell Hotel, once spread across what is now the road from Orford Place to Castle Meadow. It was demolished to make way for the new tram system installed in Norwich at the turn of the century.

Norwich Electric Tramways Company tram on Earlham Road, *c.* 1905. Trams formally came to Norwich in 1900. Over fifty worked the system, each carrying a maximum load of fifty-two passengers. They ran at roughly ten to fifteen minute intervals, fares ranging from 1*d* to 3*d*, with concessions for workmen and children. With the coming of buses, trams were no longer practicable and the last tram ran on 10 December 1935.

This wonderful study, dated about 1895, shows St Peter's Road crowded with carriers' carts and flanked by all manner of old shops and Georgian coaching inns. This entire area, running from the top of Hay Hill, round the tower of St Peter Mancroft to the top of Gaol Hill, was demolished in the 1930s to make way for the new City Hall.

The Provision Market Place looks very spacious with all the stalls cleared away for the weekend, in this view dated about 1935. The old Municipal Buildings still stand in the centre. The police hut, to the left of the photograph, was used by Norwich City Police as their headquarters between 1911 and 1938. (Photo, Philip Standley)

The fine old facade of the Royal Exchange is blasted off as the clearance of the old rat-infested Municipal Buildings moves into its final phase, *c.* 1935. The new City Hall was opened by HM King George VI on 29 October 1938. (Photo, Les Downham)

Herbert Read's fruiterer's shop, *c.* 1910. For many years the shop traded from St Benedict's Street near Cardinal's Cap Yard. (Photo, Les Downham)

Members of King's Lynn Chamber of Trade visiting Steward & Patteson's Pockthorpe Brewery, July 1953. They are watching the beer being automatically bottled at a rate of 7,200 bottles an hour.

Joseph Catling's grocer's shop and post office at 29 Carrow Road, *c.*1900.

Pull's Ferry photographed in 1929, shortly before it closed in 1930. Still one of Norwich's best-known landmarks, it takes its name from John Pull, ferry keeper and landlord of the adjacent inn in 1796.

On 27 August 1912 seven inches of rainfall coupled with uncommonly high tides caused floods in the city. After the initial shock, the inimitable spirit of the city dwellers came to the fore and working together they pulled through. Even food deliveries managed to continue, as seen here on Orchard Street. The damage was extensive, estimated at over £100,000, and 15,300 people were made temporarily homeless.

Running behind St George's Church is Tombland Alley, pictured here in about 1910. To the left and over the archway is Augustine Steward's house. He was Mayor of Norwich in 1534, 1546 and 1556, and purchased the rock-crystal mace for the City. Undoubtedly his most turbulent period of office was in 1549 when, as deputy mayor, he had to take over from the mayor himself, who had been taken prisoner and removed from the City walls by rebels during Kett's Rebellion.

This little boy is standing on a Colman's Mustard box to see over his goat-cart from which he is selling Thompson's Hokey Pokey ice-cream, *c.* 1890. The ice-cream was served in small glasses at ha'penny a lick. Sadly it was made and served in rather unhygienic conditions, and was responsible for more epidemic illnesses than anything else except milk and water.

TOWNS

One of the only county towns of Norfolk to retain a complete defensive entrance gate is King's Lynn. The gate was built in its present form in 1520, and is pictured here in about 1903.

Agricultural machinery and stalls selling provisions stand side by side in the square on market day at East Dereham, 1911. The wooden structure visible in the background is the framework for the 'Triumphal Arch', which was constructed out of wood and painted canvas as the centre-piece of Dereham's celebrations for the coronation of HM King George V in June of that year.

People throng around the stalls in Fakenham market place, *c.* 1905. Held on Thursdays for hundreds of years, the market's most important commodities were cattle and corn; millers, maltsters and merchants from Wells, Blakeney and Brancaster regularly attended.

A very fine display of bread and pastries by the baker Harold Ernest Hawes of Neville Road and Station Road, Heacham, pictured here in September 1925.

The *Norfolk Chronicle* newspaper delivery vans numbers 3 and 4 at their Norwich Road depot, Fakenham, *c.* 1930. The paper, founded in 1761, was acquired in 1930 by Sir Thomas Cook, who moved its offices from Holt to Fakenham. Sir Thomas continued to run the newspaper until 1955, when it was sold to the Norfolk News Company (now Eastern Counties Newspapers). (Photo reproduced by kind permission of Norfolk Rural Life Museum)

Cattle being driven through Reepham market place, *c.* 1905. The old market was granted in the thirteenth century and was held for generations on Wednesdays, dealing predominantly in corn and swine. The centre of a large Anglo-Saxon estate, three churches once stood in the churchyard, each belonging to a different manor in Reepham. (Photo, Philip Standley)

St Nicholas Street, Diss, *c.* 1925, named after the old St Nicholas Church which once stood there. During the mid-nineteenth century, when Diss was described as a '. . . small but neatly built, expanding Market Town', the street was known as *Half Moon Street* after the inn which stood there, kept in those days by Timothy Buckingham.

High Street, Holt, *c.* 1910. The town has a number of fine Georgian buildings, built after much of the town was destroyed by fire on May Day in 1708. The townsfolk are nicknamed 'Holt Owls', a name which came about because of the tale about a number of locals who pushed an owl up the church water spout, expecting it to drown. The owl climbed out the other end and flew away, causing much ridicule. The nickname stuck, and the tale is now part of Norfolk folklore. (Photo, Philip Standley)

Rounce & Wortley's touring carriage in front of the Black Boys public house, Aylsham market place, *c.* 1905. Pictured when it was kept by Walter Pashley, the Black Boys was first recorded in 1655. Parson Woodforde visited the pub in 1781, and commented on his meal: 'A shabby dinner and overdone'. The day was saved by the landlord, who provided some of his own spruce beer which Woodforde drank and enjoyed, and the good parson did return again.

North Walsham market cross, *c.* 1908. The cross was built in the sixteenth century by Bishop Thirlby to replace an earlier, crumbling structure, possibly one of the marker crosses of the final battle in the Norfolk Peasants' Revolt of 1381. The cross was destroyed in the town fire of 1600 but was rebuilt in 1602. It was sold to the town along with the market rights, and renovated in 1899 when a clock was installed. It still chimes, and the edifice stands as the undoubted symbol of North Walsham today.

Ralph Ling stands proudly at the door of his newly leased chemist's shop in North Walsham, 1906. Note the window display, including a very fine selection of surgical appliances. Not only a chemist but also a pioneering local photographer, Ling's photographic views of the locality provide a priceless legacy of people, life and events at the turn of the century. (Photo, Mike Ling)

A furniture van piled high waits in front of Mobb's grocery store on the High Street, Stalham, *c.* 1908. A popular market town for locals, Stalham developed as a shopping centre for Broadland visitors too. (Photo, Basil Gowen)

The Thoroughfare at Harleston, *c.* 1910. The town takes its name from a Danish leader, Heoruwulf. This was corrupted over the years to Herolveston, and passed down to successive lords including Sir John Herolveston, notorious for quelling the insurrections in the surrounding counties during the reign of Richard II. The Victorian clock tower was built in 1873 on the site of the old Harleston St John the Baptist Chapel of Ease.

William Stoveld Stace, postmaster, his staff and postmen at Watton post office, *c.* 1904. Every large town would have a post and sorting office. The postmen, with heavily laden bicycles or parcel handcarts, would also serve the surrounding villages and sub-post offices, seven days a week, including Bank Holidays. (Photo, Philip Standley)

Church Street, Attleborough, *c.* 1909. The first turnpike in Norfolk, established in 1695, ran through here en route from Norwich to Thetford and a number of fine old coaching inns were established. However, White's 1845 Directory prophesied accurately: 'Coaches, vans etc to Norwich, London, Thetford, Cambridge etc call daily at the Inns, but they will no doubt be discontinued when the railway is opened in the summer of 1845.' (Photo, Philip Standley)

Charles Harvey Standley stands proudly in the doorway of his ironmonger's shop, 'The Little Dustpan', on Town Green, Wymondham, *c.* 1900. Charles established the shop in 1886, and it became one of Wymondham's longest surviving businesses. It was run by three successive generations of the Standley family until its closure in April 1988. (Photo, Philip Standley)

Charles Eric Norton Standley beside his Ford Model T delivery van, *c.* 1912. A licensed hawker, he and his sisters Marie, Doris and Elsie delivered hardware and paraffin from their Wymondham shop to the surrounding district. (Photo, Philip Standley)

Billy Lemon, the Wymondham milkman, *c.* 1925. No milk bottles here, the milk was sold in pints and halves, the old measuring ladles clanking together as he did his rounds. Locals would listen for the milkman's call and take out bottles and jugs to collect their daily milk.

Emma Webster of Wymondham, *c.* 1895. Remembered as a 'foul-mouthed itinerant hawker', Emma was often seen asking for hand-outs at the vicarage door. Tragically, she ended her days in Wicklewood Workhouse. (Photo, Philip Standley)

East Harling market place, *c.* 1903. Dominating the corner is the long-established ironmonger's store of William Robert Pollard, who is standing in his suit in the centre of the group along with all his staff, from his domestic driver and family motor car to the shop-boy and his bicycle. (Photo, Philip Standley)

The first shops to have standardized shop fronts were the chain of International Stores, once familiar on just about every High Street. This one is pictured at Thetford in 1925.

East Dereham Fire Brigade, 1895. For many years fire brigades were localized volunteer companies who dealt with fires using human chains and buckets, or at best hand-pumped fire engines. They only came under the jurisdiction of town councils at the turn of the century. After this, urban district councils purchased more 'modern' professional engines, and also established regular bodies of trained volunteer firemen. In 1938 the system changed again, as local fire authorities were formed under the Fire Brigade Act. (Photo, Terry Davy)

East Harling Police, under Superintendent Charles Wright, 1900. Norfolk Constabulary was formed in 1839 replacing the old 'watch'. In 1900 the ordinary constable was paid no more than £1.00 a week, and all police officers were required to be outwardly smart and to show respect to magistrates; saluting them was compulsory, but 'under no circumstances to be obsequious or servile'. All off-duty officers had to leave word where they were and any constable wishing to marry had to have his prospective bride vetted by the chief constable. (Photo reproduced by kind permission of the Norfolk Constabulary)

VILLAGES

Farthing Green, Loddon, *c.* 1910. One of the small market towns of Norfolk, Loddon had a population of 1,169 when this photograph was taken. The focal point for these smaller settlements was the village green. Here would settle the travelling fair, twice a year, just one of a number of all manner of sports and entertainments which would be staged here. During election times, crowds would gather on the greens to listen to speeches delivered from farm wagons. (Photo, Philip Standley)

Tibenham, pictured at the turn of the century. In the distance is the fifteenth-century tower of All Saints' Church. The unmetalled road clearly shows the ruts from passing carriages. The rural scene is completed by the old forge, with the blacksmith Arthur Everett outside.

Posing for the camera in front of the Crown Inn at Great Hockham, *c.* 1905. At the time the inn was kept by George Hawes. The cart driver with his whip (far left) is ready to take the regulars off on a 'beano'. No doubt the accordion and violin accompanied many a traditional country chorus that day.

Garboldisham Post Office and district postmen, *c.* 1901, when Frederick Barrett Lawrence was sub-postmaster. Before the advent of modern telecommunication, letters and telegraphs were the only means of keeping in touch and just about every village had its own sub-post office. In those days even the smallest village had two posts every day except Sunday, when there was only one. (Photo, Philip Standley)

Southery Post Office, when kept by William Warnes in 1906. Some post offices diversified; often the only 'shop' in the village, they would have trays of fresh vegetables outside and provisions inside, even clothes and hardware. When the nearest town was a number of miles away they were a Godsend for the villagers. (Photo, Philip Standley)

Cottage Laundry, Hethersett, 1905. Often ladies would 'take in' washing to earn a few extra coppers, and here that principle has been taken a step further and one of the first country laundry services has been established. Well remembered are the strings stretching across the meadows, filled with drying sheets and held up with props, and of course the smell of Reckitt's Blue catching on the breeze.

With the ever present need for seed in this agricultural area, it would have been convenient to have a seed merchant on your doorstep. John Gresham Woodcock established himself in Briston in 1842 as a grocer, draper, glass and china dealer, wine and spirit merchant and agent for the Norwich Equitable Fire Office. His 'Seed Room', pictured here in about 1894, dealt in clovers, grasses, mangels and swedes.

This charming animated scene is the main street in the village of Foulsham, *c.* 1908. Most of the buildings seen here date from after 1770 when the village was practically destroyed by a great fire, which even reduced the Church of the Holy Innocents to a burnt-out shell. The damage ran into thousands but a good collection was made across the county and a play performed at Norwich for the benefit of those who had suffered, and slowly the village and church were rebuilt.

Many of the towns and villages of Norfolk have beautifully crafted signs highlighting points of history or other interests of the area. Here we see the opening of Old Catton's sign, in honour of King George V's Silver Jubilee in 1935. The sign has a cat and a barrel or 'tun'. When sign-posts had to be taken down during the war, the cat was taken into safe keeping at St Faith's Aerodrome. Before anyone realized, it had been taken over to America, but it was returned. It soon disappeared a second time, this time to Newcastle, but once again it was returned. Unfortunately, it vanished altogether in 1952. However, all was not lost as a kind benefactor provided a new cat.

Harry Toll, the Great Ryburgh coal merchant, with boy Vestigan, who assisted on the rounds, *c.* 1904.

Sam Kerridge, the roundsman for John Maidwell Outlaw, butcher, game and poultry dealer of Pulham, Pulham St Mary and Dickleburgh, pictured in October 1909. (Photo, Robert Skinner)

The roundsmen from the dairy at Rookery Farm, Worstead, c. 1935. To reach outlying hamlets and houses horse power was not always practical or necessary, so bicycles came to the fore. At one time almost every shop had a delivery man or boy with his 'trade bike', the front wheel smaller than the back to make room for the carrier and painted panel advertising the business.

Members of the Downham Market British Red Cross Society delivering emergency food to fenland villagers in the Southery area after the 1947 floods. Caused by melting snow after the terrible winter of sub-zero temperatures, the flooding made hundreds homeless, and over 40,000 acres of fenland were affected, many of which were saturated for months afterwards.

Law and order was maintained in rural districts by county police. Sgt George Bush ran the police sub-station at Coltishall and patrolled his beat on his bicycle. The occasion when some local boys shot Sgt Bush's helmet off with a catapult is still remembered; so is the severe clip round the ear they got from both Sgt Bush and their parents! (Photo reproduced by kind permission of the Norfolk Constabulary)

The police force was established after the County Police Act of 1837, but before that law and order was kept by parish constables, and courts were presided over by local gentry. Most villages had whipping posts and stocks, like these at Haveringland, and gallows were even found at some crossroads. The stocks were used for more minor offences, the miscreant having to sit from sun up to sun down and endure being pelted with everything from rotten vegetables to mud and effluent.

TRADES & CRAFTS

Mr Mark Riseborough from East Harling, at Webb's Farm near Thetford, *c.* 1950. Mark was a blacksmith for the Eastern Counties Farmers' Co-operative Association, and took his smithy around with him in the form of a portable forge and anvil.

William Atkins's wheelwright's shop at Felmingham, *c.* 1900. The wheelwright was probably one of the busiest men in the village, and would turn his hand to just about any woodworking job, from mending carts and tumbrils to repairing or replacing scythe-sticks and hay rakes. In fact, he probably handled most of the tools and equipment used by the old country craftsmen. Wheelwrights' shops were often in close proximity to blacksmiths' forges, the smith providing the shaped metal pieces required for some of the tools. (Photo, Philip Standley)

Mr W.J. Court of Feltwell, photographed in 1951, representing a third generation of his family engaged in the harness-making business. As the use of the horse declined so did the need for harness-makers and saddlers. Although many expanded their business into cobbling and making leather goods, in most cases they were not replaced when they retired.

Mr Albert Tyler and his daughter working a linen yard winder at North Lopham, *c.* 1900. For over five hundred years the wealth of Norfolk hinged upon the wool trade. Weavers' houses, with their distinctive wide windows to let in maximum light for the hand looms, were found in just about every town and village across the county. By the end of the nineteenth century the Industrial Revolution had taken the trade to the northern cities, leaving the Norfolk industry decimated. (Photo reproduced by kind permission of the Norfolk Rural Life Museum)

Jimmy Lee, the Wymondham bill poster, at the Black Horse in Flordon, *c.* 1908. Jimmy travelled for miles around the area sticking up posters advertising all manner of local events, from auctions and markets to fairs and theatrical entertainment.

Riven oak pales being made at Bob Farman's reed-thatching and basket-making business, North Walsham, June 1953.

Men, women and children work together at William Ludkin's brick yard at Banham, *c.* 1900. The 'Norfolk Red' brick is still seen in thousands of farm buildings and dwelling houses across the county. Most towns and villages were self-sufficient with their own brick kilns; in inland areas such as these there are no deposits of stone suitable for construction, and bricks are far easier to use than the cobbles and flint available on the coast.

Builders from Blazey's on Church Street, Wymondham, *c.* 1912. Builders had some very strong superstitions, which were strictly adhered to. They would pour beer or blood over the site before a new house was built to ward off evil spirits and misfortune. When the building was completed a St Andrew's cross was etched into the brickwork with a dot between each of the arms to avert the evil eye, and zig-zags were scratched on chimneys to guard against lightning strikes.

A group of Norfolk painters, *c.* 1910. Note the innovative device for painting tall window frames, third from the right. One of the painters' traditions was to dip their hands in water or splash paint on one hand before commencing, to guard against the paint in the pot drying before the job was done.

The roof of Salhouse Church being re-thatched, a job keenly observed by the vicar, Revd B.P. Luscombe, October 1953. The last time it had been completely re-thatched was ninety years previously. The work on this occasion, as then, was carried out by Farmans of North Walsham.

A sawyer and his pitman at William Crane's timber merchants, implement-makers and bell-hangers at Great Francham, *c.* 1905. The saws had long blades, as in the photograph, and a handle at both ends, one on top and one underneath. The sawyers would saw a trunk by laying it across a pit and slowly forcing the blade of the saw end to end along its length.

Steam-driven sawing equipment in action at Ketteringham, *c.* 1910. The machinery belonged to the long-established contractor Arthur John Farrow, of Mattishall. The blade on the table was spun by the traction engine, enabling large amounts of wood to be cut by a far more portable means than ever before. Where necessary wood could even be cut to length on site.

A Norfolk warrener, wearing his buskins and knee protectors, *c.* 1890. His prey lies beside him, along with the tools of his trade, a spade and a good dog. He would also use a number of gin traps and snares. The warrener's job was essential to prevent serious damage to crops in the days before myxomatosis, when the countryside was riddled with rabbits.

One of Hobrough's divers stands ready to explore the channel at Acle Bridge before dredging commences, *c.* 1900. James Hobrough & Son, the steam- and hand-dredging contractors, were established in Norwich in 1854. They also offered services such as pile driving and lighterage, as well as hiring out their steam winch, crabs and pumps 'on moderate terms' from their yard near Bishop Bridge or the dockyard at Thorpe St Andrew.

THE BIG HOUSE

Holkham Hall, one of the finest mansions in the county, was built between 1734 and 1760 and set in 3,200 acres. At one time it was the seat of Thomas William Coke, Earl of Leicester, who was one of the leading figures of the nineteenth-century agrarian revolution.

Almshouses at the entrance to Holkham Park Estate, *c.* 1905. Founded in 1757 by the Countess of Leicester at a cost of about £2,300 and endowed with a sum of £50 a year charged to the estate, the almshouses were occupied by three men and three women. They were supplied with coals, faggots, bedding and clothing, along with a gift of 6*d* a week spending money.

Westwick Arch, *c.* 1905. Built about 1780, the arch marked the entrance to the Berney estate and was also a very fine dovecote. After the diversion of the Norwich to North Walsham turnpike the arch straddled the road and a lodge was built on each side. The arch was demolished in 1981 amid much public outcry.

A group at Gunton Park, photographed on the day Colonel Harbord returned from the Boer War in October 1902. Back row, left to right: Asserton Harbord, Lord Hillingdon, Ruby Carrington, Lord Carrington, Melton Astley, Lord Hastings, Sir Richard Musgrave, Sir Frederick Sullivan. Second row: Lady Hillingdon, unknown (standing behind), Lady Carrington, Lady Keppel and Anne, Evelyn Harbord, Lady Musgrave, Philip Harbord (boy in soldier uniform), Mrs Glyn Musgrave, Lady Sullivan, Lady Hastings, Hester Harvey, Gwendolen Glyn, Lady Burroughes. Front row: Colonel Sir Charles Harbord, Lady Harbord, Toby Harbord (in sailor suit). (Photo, John Nockells)

Staff at Wood Rising Hall, *c.* 1905. Back row, left to right: Jack Smith (gardener), Herbert Wilson (underkeeper), John Milk (batboy), 'Scrimper' Ward (gardener), Cecil Lister (underkeeper), Arthur Quantrill (head gamekeeper), Miss Florence Atmore (kitchen maid), unknown. Second row: the butler, the housekeeper, Harriett Julia Russell (head housemaid), Lilly Grounds (under housemaid), unknown. Front row: Stephen King (groom), Thomas Adderson (groom), Duke the spaniel, Walter Matthews (groom). (Photo reproduced by kind permission of Norfolk Rural Life Museum)

Maids and gardeners with their Norwich-made Ransome lawnmower at a Norfolk hall, *c.* 1905. The Edwardian household gardener had to be skilled in numerous gardening practices ranging from topiary and glasshouses to herb gardens and ornamental vegetables.

Samuel Massingham, pictured with his dog Boss, 1911. Samuel was gamekeeper for the Rippingall family at Langham Hall for fifty years.

Gamekeepers under William Keeler, head gamekeeper, at the 1,000 acre Bylaugh Park Estate, home of William D'Arcy Knox Esq., *c.* 1907. During the nineteenth century 'The Black Act' made poaching punishable by death. This was repealed in 1823 and replaced by sentences of three years' hard labour or seven years' transportation. These harsh punishments caused poachers, often desperate for food, to hunt in armed gangs, making the gamekeepers' job a very dangerous occupation. Life improved as time passed, but even today poaching continues. Although on a much smaller scale, it is still an often costly irritation for the landowner.

A few pheasants have been bagged even before sitting down to this fine spread of a shoot breakfast at Bylaugh Park, *c.* 1905. This was one of the most popular pastimes of the gentry, around five hundred pheasants and four hundred hares and rabbits considered a good 'bag' for a day's shoot.

The west front and terrace of Sandringham House, *c.* 1922. Built in 1870 to designs by A.J. Humbert, the London architect, and set in an estate covering over 15,578 acres, the house has been the popular Norfolk retreat of successive monarchs since Queen Victoria. (Photo, Pamela Standley)

Glasshouses and the head gardener's house at Sandringham, *c.* 1903. At this time the position was held by Archibald Mackellar. The extensive gardens were kept by a huge team of skilled gardeners; among them in the late thirties, when Charles Cook was head gardener, was a young Percy Thrower, who became known to a generation as 'The Television Gardener'. (Photo, Mary Standley)

The kennels at Sandringham, *c.* 1911. William Brunsdon, the kennel keeper, is pictured with the favourite Pomeranian dog of King George V's children. (Photo, Pamela Standley)

Their Majesties King Edward VII, Queen Alexandra, and the King of Portugal among a royal shooting party at Sandringham, *c.* 1907. (Photo, Mary Standley)

THE COAST

Landing a big catch on the quay at Wells, *c.* 1908. (Photo, Eric Reading)

King's Lynn docks, *c.* 1878. Sea trade in Lynn goes back over a thousand years; indeed it was the third most important port in England in about 1200. The docks as we know them today date from the late 1800s. The Prince of Wales opened the Alexandra Dock in 1869, and Bentinck Dock was opened in 1883.

Hunstanton beach, *c.* 1910. Small pleasure yachts skirt the waters and people stroll along the beach. In the background, stretching 800 feet out to sea, is the old Hunstanton Pier, built in 1870. (Photo, Philip Standley)

Miss Constance Knipe, Lady Superintendent, and her resident girls at the Girls' Friendly Society Home of Rest at Freiburg House on Avenue Road, Hunstanton, 1913.

The east end of Wells harbour, *c.* 1907. In the nearest boat, with his dog and shotgun, is Percy Barnett, the local boatman, no doubt ready for one of his duck or goose shoots. Once a busy port predominantly exporting malt, Wells also had a fine fishing and oyster industry which sadly dwindled away at the turn of the century. Its dock, built in 1859 by the Earl of Leicester, spreads due north from the west end of the quay, straightening the once tortuous channel to the quay, which caused the old ships to have to discharge their loads into lighters in the pool by the lighthouse. (Photo, Eric Reading)

Fishermen young and old sit mardling on Blakeney quay, *c.* 1927. In the Middle Ages Blakeney was a thriving port, trading in wool and fish, and later grain. However, nature itself worked against the future of the port as the tides continually carried the spit of land at Blakeney Point further west until the channel silted up. It is now over 4 miles from the quay to the open sea.

The Dun Cow at Salthouse, as familiar today as when this photograph was taken in about 1903, when the inn was kept by Walter Graveling. Walter also ran his blacksmith's shop nearby. Salthouse was once a busy port on the 'Mayne Channel' from Blakeney, but embankments built in the seventeenth and eighteenth centuries blocked it. The village is under constant threat from the sea and many houses have been simply washed away; a lady was even killed here during floods in 1953. (Photo, Philip Standley)

Fishermen and their boats on the east beach at Sheringham, *c.* 1955. About this time Sheringham had thirty-five boats employed in the fishing industry, their catch comprising herring, cod, skate, plaice, crab, lobster and whelks. The fishermen were a final reminder of the little fishing hamlet, squeezed out by the hotels, shops and new streets of the seaside resort it developed into during the 1890s.

Cromer, seen from the East Cliffs, *c.* 1900. Known as the 'Gem of the Norfolk Coast', Cromer was a fashionable bathing place from the late 1820s. However, its heyday, like that of Sheringham, came during the late Victorian period with the coming of the railway, continuing into the Edwardian period when many of its distinctive hotels and guest houses were built. The pier, extending 183 yards, was constructed in 1899 at a cost of £11,000, and a continuation of the promenade at £34,000.

The Cromer lifeboat *Harriot Dixon* with her crew. Left to right: Frank Davies, Leslie 'Yacker' Harrison, Joe Linder (No. 2 Mechanic), George Cox, Henry 'Shrimp' Davies, Billy 'Plimpo' Davies, Jimmy Davies, Jack Davies, Leslie Harrison, William 'Captain' Davies, Henry Blogg (Coxswain), Tom 'Bussey' Allen, Robert 'Skinback' Cox, Arthur Balls, Walter Burgess, George Balls, Bob Davies. (Photo, Philip Standley)

Cromer lighthouse, situated 250 feet high on the East Cliffs, *c.* 1905. The first lighthouse was built in 1719, replacing a beacon which used to be lit on top of the church tower. The original lighthouse stood on a hill in front of this one; it was lit by coal, and was turned by a clockwork mechanism and kept alight with mighty bellows. Sadly, it was lost in 1866 when the land on which it stood succumbed to coastal erosion. In anticipation of this event, Trinity House had this replacement built in 1832. It has an electric light of 49,000 candle power, and on a clear day can be seen from almost 23 miles out to sea.

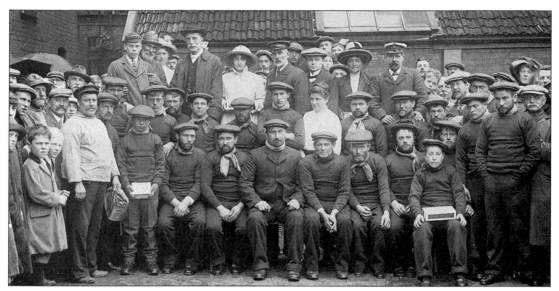

The Cromer fisherfolk with the recently rescued crew of the Belgian fishing vessel *St Antoine de Padoue*, pictured in the yard of the Red Lion, August 1912. The fisherfolk were a close 'family' community, hard-working and with their own traditions and superstitions. Many would tell of the fine port of Shipden, which stood between Cromer and the sea and was washed away in the fourteenth century. The great 'Church Rock' of Shipden, a real hazard to shipping, survived but was eventually blown up; it is said that above the squall on dark stormy nights can still be heard the spectral booming of Shipden Church bells. (Photo, Philip Standley)

'The Garden of Sleep', *c*. 1900. This was in fact the tower of St Michael's Church at Sidestrand, in its unique setting on the cliff edge surrounded by poppies. It was popularized by Clement Scott in his column entitled 'Poppyland'; the name struck for the area and 'The Garden of Sleep' for its idyllic heart. Ironically, when the flower of English manhood was being slaughtered on the Somme in 1916, the tower slipped over the edge; nothing was quite the same again.

The Church of All Saints at Mundesley, seen here in its ruinous state, *c.* 1885. Despite its appearance at this date it was still described as a '. . . little church within a church with a pyramid roof'. However, it was restored in 1903–4 under the guidance of the Revd Thomas Tegg Harvey. A new organ, choir stall and fittings were provided, paid for by public subscription and benevolent donations from local gentry.

Mending nets on Bacton beach, *c.* 1926. This small village on the north Norfolk coast combines the two hamlets of Bacton Green and Bromholme, and has a population of about seven hundred. A Cluniac priory was founded in Bromholme in 1113, visited by many pilgrims travelling to see the Holy Rood of Bromholme.

The Happisburgh lifeboat *Jacob and Rachel Valentine*, being pulled into action by a ten-horse team from Love's Farm, *c.* 1909. The boat served Happisburgh between 1907 and 1926. She was launched sixteen times and saved nineteen lives.

Happisburgh lighthouse, *c.* 1910. It was built in 1791 and originally powered by candles. The distinctive red bands, visible for miles around, were painted on in 1883 when occulting light was installed. Electricity was eventually installed in 1942.

Another reminder of our constant battle against coastal erosion: the tower of St Mary's Church, Eccles, *c.* 1890. Once a noted fishing town of 2,000 acres, all but a few of Eccles's houses have been swept away by the sea. This last monument of the town that was, was itself swept away after a storm in 1895.

Sea Palling, *c.* 1910. The old boy was probably on his way to the beach to help draw in the catch, and maybe let a few of the children have a ride on his hard-working donkey. Sea Palling has always been a quiet coastal village; when this photograph was taken the population was about four hundred.

Newport, pictured *c.* 1950, along with the hamlets of Scratby and California in Ormesby St Michael perpetuate the almost continuous coast-line development of holiday residences from Great Yarmouth to Winterton. Buildings began to appear at the turn of the century but the majority of the holiday camps and chalet parks were set up in the late 1950s and '60s when this area was at its most popular.

The Caistor Lifeboat Memorial commemorating the disaster in 1903 when nine crewmen lost their lives when their boat capsized. James Haylett, a 78-year-old ex-coxswain, pulled the only two survivors from the water. He is credited as saying at the inquest: 'Caistor men never turn back.' However, what he actually said was an even greater tribute to the crewmen. When asked if they had considered giving up, James replied: 'No, they never give up. They could have been there until this time if they could have held on. Coming back is against the rules when we see signals like that.'

Tall ships fill Hall quay, Great Yarmouth, *c.* 1887. In 1724 Daniel Defoe said that Great Yarmouth 'is an antient town' and truly it is. From its origins as a small fishermen's settlement on a sandbank, it developed after the Roman occupation, building up trade on the worth of its wool. It eventually became the eighth most important port of England.

The Princess Mary charabanc in front of the Sailors' Home on Marine Parade, Great Yarmouth, *c.* 1920. A 3*s* 6*d* return ticket took you on a tour of Broadland including Horning Ferry, Ormesby Broads, Potter Heigham and Fleggburgh. (Photo, Eddie Riseborough)

Crowds of holiday-makers and day-trippers at Britannia Pier, Great Yarmouth, *c.* 1935. Built for the first time in 1858, it burnt down but was rebuilt in 1902 at a cost of £65,000. In 1910 the pavilion burnt down, but another was rebuilt to seat 1,400 people. The pier and its attractions are still as popular today.

Goodman's Pierrots, who did the Norfolk circuit in the years between 1909 and the beginning of the First World War. No trip to the coast, especially Great Yarmouth, would have been complete without visiting an end of the pier show with entertainment from a travelling Pierrot troupe like this.

Another treat was to have shellfish like cockles or whelks, bought on small china dishes which you returned to the vendor when you had finished. This stall, pictured in about 1910, was run on the beach for many years by George Holmes. George also had a wet fish shop at 20 George Street, Great Yarmouth. (Photo, Philip Standley)

Gorleston beach, *c.* 1905. Couples promenade along the beach, ladies with parasols and men in their straw boaters on this beautiful Edwardian sunny day. Tents for changing and bathing machines to allow discreet entry into the sea are lined up along the beach; it was considered quite vulgar to be seen out of the water in a bathing costume. (Photo, Sarah Standley)

Steam and sail drifters pulling out of Gorleston harbour, *c.* 1910. Over a thousand boats sailed out during the herring season, which ran from September to the middle of December. In the days before the Second World War upward of five hundred thousand cran would have been caught. The effects of the world wars and indiscriminate fishing by other countries prevented any real recovery after the war, and those 'herring heydays' had passed into history by the late 1960s.

Drifters return to Great Yarmouth on a Monday morning, *c.* 1920. Smoke from the funnels would create a smog over the town as the herring was unloaded in swills on the wharf, counted by tellers in bowler hats and then auctioned. The catch was then piled onto carts and lorries and taken to the cutting and curing yards. (Photo, Philip Standley)

Scots fisher girls, *c.* 1920. Coming down on trains from the northern ports, the girls followed the herring fleet and worked gutting the thousands of fish landed in the season. They very rarely wore gloves for the job and never appeared idle. While waiting for the next catch they could be seen walking in groups, knitting as they went along.

EVENTS & OCCASIONS

The opening of Lynn Mart, the traditional start of the Norfolk fair circuit, held as always on 14 February. This ceremony, on Wednesday 14 February 1912, was performed by the Mayor, Mr F.R. Floyd, and was followed by a speech from Mr Holcombe Ingleby, the local MP. However, music from the organs which had started playing after the mayor's opening message drowned out his voice and he abandoned the effort.

May Day celebrations round the maypole at Colkirk, *c.* 1910. The origins of the May Day celebrations can be traced back to the Celtic festival of Beltane, marking the beginning of summer. 'May' itself was gathered at sunrise and could be any kind of flowering greenery. As seen here it was then bound round the pole and sealed with the gay ribbons in the dance. (Photo, Philip Standley)

Marchers gather at Banham for the Oak Apple Day parade, *c.* 1880. Led by the band and with members of the Ancient Order of Foresters prominent in the procession, such events were once common across the country. They were held to commemorate the restoration of King Charles II on 29 May 1660.

Whit Monday sports at King's Head Meadow, Wymondham, *c.* 1894. At this time of year sporting events were popular in villages and towns across the county. All ages enjoyed the fun, from youngsters knocking each other off a pole with stuffed sacks to the veterans' egg and spoon race. No doubt such events were the source of many laughs at the local pub for months after. (Photo, Philip Standley)

Hospital Sunday parade in East Dereham market place, *c.* 1910. A popular event held in most towns across the county before the creation of the National Health Service, when hospitals were maintained by charitable donations, 'Hospital Sunday' would involve a big parade and fête to raise money for the local cottage hospital. (Photo, Terry Davy)

Watton and District Liberal Club at election time, *c.* 1910. Posters demanding Free Trade are displayed on the building. At least the elections were more orderly than when the 'Orange and Purples' (Tories) and 'Blue and Whites' (Whigs) hotly contested county elections. Often politically biased public houses were situated not far apart, and would display the state of the poll outside their doors. This inevitably led to fights and often full-scale riots would break out and the local militia would have to be called in to disperse the crowds. (Photo, Philip Standley)

The circus bandwagon draws a crowd at Walsingham, *c.* 1895. Apart from the traditional twice-yearly fairs, travelling circuses would often visit country towns and villages. Their arrival was always heralded by gaily coloured caravans led by the bandwagon, which would return to drum up punters for the show.

Foulsham fair, 1909. Foulsham fair, 'for cattle and pleasure', was typical of the country fairs held across the county on dates set since time immemorial. In Foulsham's case, the date was always the first Tuesday in May.

Tombland fair, 1907. The fair took its original name from the area in which it was held from the twelfth century to the early nineteenth. However, since 1818, after complaints about noise and disruption were upheld in court, the fair has been held every Christmas and Easter on Castle Meadow, Agricultural Hall Plain and the old cattle market, now the Castle Mall Shopping Centre.

A whole ox being roasted at the Great Yarmouth Christmas fair, 1905. Ox roasts were once common features of hiring fairs, events where farm workers, tradesmen and domestic servants would seek employment. They would wear or carry a representation of their trade, for example, a spade or a mop, to indicate to prospective employers just what their trade was. (Photo, Philip Standley)

Hundreds of choristers fill the hall at a ceremony which was the culmination of the pageantry organized to welcome the new King George V and Queen Mary on 8 November 1910. King's Lynn held the honour of being the first town to address King George V and Queen Mary as new monarchs. (Photo, Mary Standley)

The Union Flag has been hoisted and hymns are sung to commence the celebrations at Loddon in honour of the coronation of HM King George V on 22 June 1911.

Many towns and villages across the county organized open-air dinners to celebrate King George V's coronation in 1911. After many months of planning, and the construction of countless trestle tables, 3,100 diners sat down to consume 213 stone of beef, £6 2s 8d worth of pickles and vinegar, 100 stone of bread and 78 stone of special Coronation Cake, washed down with 144 gallons of beer and 7½ barrels of ginger beer.

Festivities in Hingham, 11 August 1913, when a memorial tablet was presented from the inhabitants of Hingham in Massachusetts, USA. Samuel Lincoln, an ancestor of the American president, emigrated to America from Hingham in 1637. A bust of Abraham Lincoln was unveiled in the parish church by John Davis, the American ambassador, in 1919. (Photo, Philip Standley)

Nurses man a stall to raise money for the Soldiers' Comfort Fund and Harleston Red Cross Hospital during the First World War. As popular today as years ago, fetes and galas are quite typical of English summer days. Many of yesteryear's events would have taken place on the lawn of the local 'Big House'.

PASTIMES & LEISURE

Arthur Reeve, the blacksmith, mardles with friends Charlie Goodman and Dan Filley at the smithy at New Buckenham, 1950. Probably the most popular pastime and recreation in Norfolk, 'mardling' means to talk about anything and everything, honestly and with that unique and endearing Norfolk wit and wisdom.

1st Stalham Scout Troop in the school yard, 1910. The uniforms they wear are very similar to those of the South African Constabulary, which Robert Baden-Powell, the founder of the scout movement, commanded during the South African War 1899–1902. The staves, carried at one time by all scouts, were not only used for everything from making the side of a stretcher to judging distances, but were also carved with various symbols of that scout's personal achievements as he progressed through the movement.

Stibbard Girl Guides stand proudly beside their collection of paper salvage for the War Effort, August 1940.

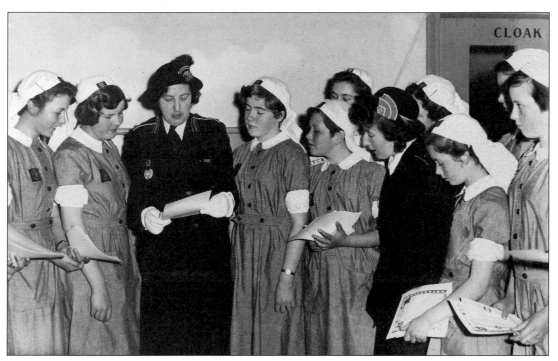

The long-serving, well-remembered and respected Mrs Anne Ettridge, Norfolk County Staff Officer for St John Ambulance Cadets, reads the citation for the presentation of First Air exam passes at North Walsham Quadrilateral Division's Annual General Meeting in 1957.

Boys' Brigade sergeants, complete with sun-hats, at County Camp held at Mundesley-on-Sea, 1913. (Photo, Eric Reading)

Nothing can be more evocative of the halcyon days of England in high summer than the sound of leather on willow echoing from the village green. Here we see members of the King's Own Royal Regiment Norfolk Yeomanry cricket team on Holkham Park cricket ground in August 1914, the first month of the First World War. I can't help wondering how many came home to play again. (Photo, Philip Standley)

Brothers Don and Ernie Griffin having a 'knock-about' on the lawn at River Farm, Honing. At one time just about every country boy had a pair of boxing gloves, and trained by punching the dust out of the hearth rug hung on the washing line or sparring with friends. The highlight of the week would be cycling to the local Lads' Club for gym training and competition sparring. This produced a number of national champions from the county, such as the legendary 'Ginger' Sadd. It also meant a surprise or two for some of the old prizefighters at travelling fairs, when the local boy did go three rounds and received his 10 bob reward.

Paston Football Club, 1925/6. The game of football became popular in the fourteenth century. To begin with the rules were flexible; teams numbered ten or twelve, and the pitch could be up to 200 yards long. The ball was shaped a little like a rugby ball, the player in possession running with it towards the opponent's goal and only kicking it when he was pressed. Boots were tipped with horn, hardened with blood; one eighteenth-century account describes how 'the contest for the ball begins and never ends without black eyes and bloody noses'.

Dereham Ladies' hockey club, Norfolk Tournament Winners, 1928/9. Back row, left to right: L. Read, F. Wilson, E. Rowe, B. Robinson, M. Howes. Front row: K. Read, E. Wilson, V. Clarke, M. Eade, C. Robinson. (Photo, Terry Davy)

Members of North Walsham Private Bowls Club, *c.* 1930. The game of bowls was once frowned on by the State because people began to prefer it to archery, upon which rested the military spirit of the county. Weathering the ages, many towns and villages still have proudly tended greens today.

Briningham White Horse quoits team, winners of the hotly contested Norfolk Quoits League, 1925/6. Sadly, interest in the game of quoits has greatly declined, and today it is really only seen at the more rural county shows.

Model boats on the boating lake at Gorleston, *c.* 1925. The making of model boats is a timeless pastime, although at this point 'all-in' model kits were still a thing of the future; most of the boats seen here would have been constructed from scratch using authentic materials.

A father and son out fishing 'after the wily pike', at Decoy Corner, East Harling, *c.* 1910.

The shoot has been a popular pastime for generations, as well as a good way to keep down the destructive pigeon population. Gathered here are 'The Guns', many with their faithful gun-dogs, ready for the shoot at Woodrow Farm, Moulton, in 1909.

A hare coursing meet at Pulham St Mary, *c.* 1910. The countryman of old, be he gentry or plebeian, derived much entertainment from hunting or killing animals for sport.

The Norwich Stag Hounds and hunt entourage near Eaton, 1910. The meet was once a common sight, the local squire mustering the hunters in their pinks in the local square. The pastime was not really popular with locals as the hunt would often trample across the cropped fields of the squires' tenant farmers or even charge through cottage gardens.

The Lord Mayor of Norwich's swan-upping party after an afternoon's trapping on the Wensum near Norwich, *c.* 1916. Swan-upping, which took place every August, was the process of catching swans and establishing their ownership by noting any distinctive 'swan marks', or cutting nicks in the bill if the birds were cygnets. The men who made these cuts were called 'uppers'. From the number caught, a few cygnets were taken to the old swan pit at the Great Hospital in Norwich, where they were fattened up for the Mayoral Banquet at Christmas.

Castle Acre 'Nelson' Band, *c.* 1900. It was Sunday Best all round and proudly polished instruments for the village and town bands of yesteryear, sadly an unfamiliar sight nowadays.

The Harleston Orchestra ready for its performance at the Smoking Concert, held at the local Corn Hall, 1912. Such performances were frequently organized and often involved many members of the local community. Acts ranged from monologues and funny stories to dancing and singing.

Hingham 'Nigger Minstrels', *c.* 1910. Obviously not politically correct now, but a song or two from a black-faced minstrel troupe was a popular feature of any entertainment evening in the early 1900s.

As bicycles became available (often purchased via the local hardware store or blacksmith) so cycling clubs were set up, like this one at Docking, pictured in about 1910. Often based at local inns, the cyclists would tour the area, visiting the respective village pubs as they passed through. It is a good thing our roads were so much quieter in those days, as they wobbled home after supping a few pints of good country ale, although no doubt many of their number ended up in ditches.

Worstead 'New Inn' darts team, April 1954. A comparatively modern addition to pub entertainments, darts was a spin-off from archery, an ancient skill once practised in every town and village. Indeed, for many generations the law decreed that every man must practise archery on a Sunday. Archery may have declined, but darts matches are still played in local pubs most evenings, let alone just Sundays.

Play or knock? Dominoes are played before an intent audience at Walsingham, November 1951. No doubt the pungent smell of shag tobacco mixed with the aroma of real country ale set the atmosphere for an evening of games and mardling about crops, poaching and the weather – real country life in the heart of Norfolk.

THE MILITARY & WAR

Members of the Norfolk Rifle Volunteers on summer training camp at Great Yarmouth, *c.* 1869. The popularity of local volunteer regiments was proved by just about every village and town across the county having its own detachment or company. They used corn halls for drill, and held 'candle practice' when candles were used as targets. No ammunition was used, the air shooting out of the percussion cap rifles snuffing out the flame.

Squadron sergeant and troopers of the King's Own Royal Regiment, Norfolk Imperial Yeomanry, 1905. They are wearing the fine blue field dress jacket and pantaloons introduced that year, although they have retained the distinctive shoulder chains and brass accoutrements. Norfolk being the farming county it is, the yeomanry was never short of mounts, and recruits were keen to be part of the remarkable spectacle of the regiment.

Territorials of the 5th Battalion, the Norfolk Regiment, fall in for Sunday Church Parade at Downham in August 1912. Known as the 'Saturday Night Soldiers', the local men served with their local detachments at weekends and away at summer camp. Their skills were often displayed on such parades and 'Field Days' in the days before the First World War.

Bugles and drums add to the patriotic fervour as the local Territorial boys line up at Hunstanton station on Wednesday 5 August, the morning after war was declared, waiting for the trains which would take them to their war stations. Many of these young lads would never return home, losing their lives in the carnage and disease of the Dardanelles and Mesopotamia.

Not quite sure what to make of it, curious onlookers and members of the 3rd (Reserve) Battalion, the Norfolk Regiment, on Crown Road, Great Yarmouth, examine one of the bombs dropped in the Zeppelin air raid on 19 January 1915. It was in fact the first aerial bombing raid ever. Carried out by two airships, the first bomb was dropped on Sheringham causing only minimal damage. However, the first fatal casualties were incurred in Great Yarmouth and King's Lynn.

Soon after war was declared, Norfolk was filled with military encampments in every spare large building and on every piece of open land, be it fallow fields or estate. Here are members of the Glamorgan Imperial Yeomanry at some of their commandeered stabling in Aylsham, January 1915.

The local vet has been called in to treat one of the mounts of the 1/2 Derbyshire Yeomanry when they were stationed in East Dereham during 1915.

Nurses and recuperating servicemen in the casualty shed at the Norfolk and Norwich Hospital, 1915. The horrific numbers of casualties brought to the county soon filled the hospitals, and tents and sheds like these were erected in the grounds to cope with the overspill. Soon even these became inadequate and large houses across the county were 'commandeered' as Voluntary Aid Detachment Hospitals for convalescing troops.

The inauguration of East Ruston War Memorial, erected in memory of the nineteen men of the village who were killed in the First World War. In rural communities such as these the effects of the war were often deeply felt, villages decimated by the loss of so many of their young men. Of those who did return, many were disabled in body or mind. Things were never the same again.

Collectors for Norwich's first Earl Haig Fund Poppy Day, held in November 1921. Over a hundred thousand Norfolk men fought in the First World War; one in nine did not return, and everybody was affected. The first Norfolk Poppy Day raised £106,000 for the benefit of widows, orphans and the estimated five hundred thousand disabled British ex-servicemen.

The band of the 5th Battalion, the Norfolk Regiment, June 1927. Led by Bandmaster Dines (far right), the band was a popular feature at parades and events. That year, it played at the Sandringham Flower Show, at West Runton, and at Cromer during the annual camp. At the King's Lynn Community Singing Event, the clarinet player had to be attended to as, while joining in the chorus of 'John Peel', he dislocated his larynx.

Assembling gas masks at Wells, 1939. Poison gas was used for the first time on the Western Front in 1915; its horrific effects were well remembered by all who suffered from or witnessed them. With the threat of gas being dropped on to civilian targets, strict guidelines were set out and precautions planned. Since the mid-1930s Air Raid Precautions Committees were set up in each region to start training programmes which included use of the stirrup pump, first aid, gas training and how to extinguish incendiary bombs. Many members of the public who attended these sessions went on to become members of the Civil Defence. (Photograph reproduced by kind permission of Norfolk Rural Life Museum)

Men of Saxthorpe and Corpusty Platoon, Norfolk Home Guard, *c.* 1941. On 14 May 1940 Sir Anthony Eden, Secretary of State for War, appealed over the radio for men aged between seventeen and sixty-five and for whatever reason not engaged in military service to join the Local Defence Volunteers, later known as the Home Guard. As Norfolk was an agricultural county, many men were exempt from war service as they were in 'reserved occupations', working on the farms and producing food. However, many wanted to do something for their country and joining the Home Guard offered them that opportunity. They were keenly patriotic and, along with those too old or too young to sign up for regular forces but who could also join the Home Guard, they formed seventeen battalions of volunteers. Their duties ranged from guarding railway lines and water towers to patrolling their duty area, especially to look out for German paratroopers.

His Majesty King George VI, accompanied by Lieut. Col. J.H. Jewson MC, TD inspects members of the 4th Battalion, Royal Norfolk Regiment TA, at Gorleston where they were on coastal defence duty, 23 August 1940. Most of these men served their duty here through one of the coldest winters on record, only to be plummeted into the débâcle that was Singapore in 1941/2, consequently enduring unimaginable hardships and degradations for the duration of the war as prisoners in Japanese hands. Many never saw again the county they loved. (Photo reproduced by kind permission of the Imperial War Museum; H3258)

Storming the cliffs, ducking live ammunition fire at Cromer, 1942. Such exercises were carried out across the county by soldiers from many regiments. The training on the Norfolk terrain proved to be excellent preparation for the campaigns in North-West Europe in 1944. (Photo reproduced by kind permission of the Imperial War Museum; H18934)

Pilot Officer Cecil Thomas Kingsborough Cody being chaired to the mess by members of his squadron at RAF Coltishall, 1943. It was the day of the visit of King George VI and Queen Elizabeth to the station, and ten minutes before the arrival of the royal party the fighters had scrambled – 'Enemy aircraft approaching'. This twenty-year-old Irish-born pilot secured his first kill shortly after. Describing his incredible engagement with the Ju88 to their Majesties, he was warmly congratulated. (Photo reproduced by kind permission of the Imperial War Museum; CH8402)

Airmen and ground crew of 'Blonds Away' at USAAF Station 114 at Hethel, 1943. This was one of the first of many heavy bomber bases built in the county during the Second World War. When this photograph was taken, the base was home to 389 Bomb Group, who flew the first active mission from here on 7 September 1943. In fact, over three hundred missions were undertaken from Hethel before the end of hostilities, their Liberators and those from other bases once a familiar sight in the Norfolk skies.

Firemen anxiously pull their trailer pump to attend a fire on Rampant Horse Street in the aftermath of the blitz on Norwich, 28 April 1942. The county saw much bombing but probably the worst was on the nights of 27/8 and 29/30 April 1942, when Hitler launched his 'Baedeker Blitz' aimed at the historical cities of England. Some people believed the end of the world had come. (Photo reproduced by kind permission of Eastern Counties Newspapers)

VE-Day celebrations at Binham, 8 May 1945. Often these small celebrations hold more poignancy than those in the cities and towns because of the amount of effort the small villages put into their special event. No doubt many of these children had to wait quite a bit longer before Daddy came home. Victory over Japan and the complete end of hostilities on 15 August was still two long months away.

In the post-war years thousands of Norfolk men were called up for National Service, and many went into their county regiment. Here, after six weeks' training, the Royal Norfolk Regiment march past Sir Edmund Bacon, Lord Lieutenant of Norfolk, at their passing-out parade at Britannia Barracks in May 1952. (Photo reproduced by kind permission of Eastern Counties Newspapers)

ACKNOWLEDGEMENTS & INDEX

The author gratefully acknowledges the following, without whom this book would not have been possible: Terry Davy; Les Downham; Eastern Counties Newspapers and ECN Library Staff; George Gosling; Basil Gowen; Fred Griffin; George Hill; the Imperial War Museum; Mike Ling; The M& GN Circle; John Nockells; Norwich Central Library Local Studies Department; Norfolk Rural Life Museum, Gressenhall; Eric Reading; Eddie Riseborough; Robert Skinner; Pamela Standley; Philip and Mary Standley.

I am grateful yet again to Terry Burchell, for photographic wonders, and my heartfelt thanks go to all those who have supported and encouraged my research over the years.

Finally but certainly by no means least, my thanks go to my family for their endless support and encouragement but especially to my darling Sarah for her assistance in additional research, her support and love for this temperamental author.

Every attempt has been made in this book to obtain permission from copyright holders to reproduce their photographs and to acknowledge them. However, because of the age and anonymity of some of the photographers or publishers it has not be possible to trace all the details. Please accept my apologies; no breach of those rights was intended.